book-Cover

The cultural heritage of shreeNathdwara

Yashwant kothari

THE CULTURAL HERI TAGE OF SHREE NATHDWARA (SHREE NATHJI)

YASHWANT KOTHARI
86, LAXMI NAGAR
O/S BRAHAM PURI
JAIPUR-302002

Preface

Shree Nathdwara is the place where I was born some SIXTY years ago, but much Water has flown through the Banas river since than. I have been working on the cultural heritage of shree Nathdwara since long. I have read a number of books and articles published, I my self surveyed the town several times alone and with friends in my early child hood, And after time and again.

Shree Nathdwara has always attracted me from my childhood. I am living in jaipur. But my heart lives in shree Nathdwara and in charan kamal of shree nathji. I tried my level best to travel Shree Nathdwara as much as I can but unfortunately I got little time out of my family affairs and job, to visit shree Nathdwara.

The idea to write a book on the cultural heritage of Shree Nathdwara is not new to me, Because as far as I know not a single book on this topic is available. A few scattered works are in Hindi or are like a tourist guide book only.

So, I finally decided to work on this project but it took much time, I wrote it in pieces, got it corrected as far as possible, went through the available literature, corrected the manuscript, How ever still there can be a lot of improvisation in the book, but with all it's short comings the book is in your hands, dear reader. I am thankful to all who helped me in the process of writing.

0 0 0

Deepawali

Yours
Yashwant Kothari

Contents

1-introduction
2- art , culture and craft etc -
3-pusti marg, temple, and festivals.
4-tourist spot in shree Nathdwara
5- places around shree Nathdwara
6-markets and colonies
7-places to stay
8-artists, writers, journalists, politicians
9--references

Photos-courtesy-

1-Sahitya mandal,Shree Nathdwara

2-Prabhu das vairagi

3-Girish asher

4-Temple board 5-Yashwant kothari   6-google

Dedicated in the charan kamal of lord shreenathji and to the devoties-yashwant kothari

Lord Shree Nathji

Introduction

History of Shree Nath ji Temple

When **Aurangjeb** started to ruin the **Vaishnawat temple** of north India, **Shree Nathji Swaroop** was brought to Mewar state. On the request of **Rajmata Maharana Rajsinghji** allowed the swaroop to stay at Siyad near Nathdwara. Later on a grand temple was built in Shree Nathdwara and the Swaroop was established their. Since then Shree Nathdwara is known as Pradhan Peeth of Vallabh Sampraday.

The temple is one of the best temples of the country. Shree Nathdwara is well connected by rail and road;

nearest airport is Dabok near Udaipur. Shree Nathdwara is fifty k.m. from Udaipur in north direction and is on national highway 8.

Arts

The main arts are

1. **Painting** 2. **Meenakari** 3. **Music** 4. **Tie and die**

- Paintings of Shree Nathdwara – Shree Nathdwara is known for its painters and paintings. All these paintings have Shree Nathji depictions in various forms in most of the paintings Shree Nathji is painted with bright colours and in childhood form. The paintings of Shree Nathdwara can be classified in following three categories

1. **Bhitti chitra (Wall paintings)**
Wall paintings are famous. Elephants, ladies, flowers, Peacock and such other paintings are depicted on various parts of the temple and on the men gate of the temple.

2. **Pichvai (Cloth paintings)**
Pichvai (Cloth paintings) the cloth paintings are used inside the temple and behind the swaroop. These cloth paintings are decorated by golden work, Salma Sitara etc. The cloth paintings are very costly. Apart from Shree Nathji Bhagawat is also painted on cloth.

3. **Other paintings**

the painters of Shree Nathdwara paint on leaf of Pipal, Rice, Supari, Hathi Dant, and Plastic Sheets and even on Marble pieces. The noted artists of Shree Nathdwara are Ghasiram, Sukhdev, Radheshyam, Ambalal, Dwarkaprasad, Vittaldas, Revashanker, Chiranjilal Sharma, L.M. Shrma, Inder Sharma, J.P. Sharma, B.G.

Sharma, B.M. Sharma. The paintings of Shree Nathdwara have been appreciated by forigners also. In modern art Char an Sharma and Mohan Sharma have done good work, where is Revashanker is an artist of international repute. A large numbers of calendars are also painted by Nathdwara artist. The man Swroop of Shree Nathji is painted by all artist with local colours and this is their lively hood.

- Minakari works is also famous on silver white metal on gold. The Minakari items of Shree Nathdwara are sold through out the country Ear ring, Pendls, Churi, Choti, Nosering and Paijeb are the main ornaments solds in Shree Nathdwara.
- The music of Shree Nathji temple is also very famous. Pakhavas, Haveli Sangit, Druvapad and Astachap music is resited in all the eight Jalki of Shree Nathji. The famous musicians of Shree Nathdwra are Shree Harnath Kirtankar, Purushottam das pakhavaji, Ramdas kumavat, Mulchand kumavt, Mishrilal kumavat, Prakash chand kumavat. Shree Nathji has ownband known as Shree Nath bend. It is a 100 year old bend and it plays regularly.

The tie and die industry is also very famous, saries salvar suits, chunnies, gown, angerrakhi and cloths of young boys and girls are sold on shops.

Pustimarg—pustimarg was established by Shree madvallabhaachharya. It is a way of devotion to lord Krishna .I n Shree Nathji child hood form of lord Krishna is worshiped. The Go swami Heritage of the temple is as follows
1. Shree Madvallabhacharyaji
2. Shree Vitthalnathji
3. Shree Girdhariji
4. Shree Damodarji
5. Shree Vittalrayji
6. Shree Girdhariji
7. Shree Bade Dauji
8. Shree Vitthleshji
9. Shree Goverdhaneshji
10. Shree Bade Girdhariji
11. Shree dauji
12. Shree Govindji
13. Shree Girdhariji
14. Shree Goverdhanlalji
15. Shree Damodarlalji
16. Shree Govindlalji
17. Shree Rajivji

At Present Shree Rakesh baba is Tilkayat and chief of the Shree Nathji Temple. His address is khas daftar, Moti mahal, Shree Nathdwara and Shree Vallabh darshan, Poddhar path, Santa kruj, (west), Mumbai.

Photos of goswamis of Temple:

Clock wise from top-left: Girdhariji, Goverdhanlalji, Damodarlalji and Govindlalji Majarai

-There are seven up-peeth of Shree Nathji temple-they are-

SEVEN-UP-PEETH

1. Shree Mathureshji — Kota
2. Shree Vittalnathji — Nathdwara
3. Shree Dwarkadhishji — Kankroli
4. Shree Gokulunathji — Gokul
5. Shree Gokulchandrmaji — Kamvan
6. Shree Balkrishnaji — Surat
7. Shree Madanmohanji — Kamvan

BHANDARS OF SHREE NATHJI are as under-

1. Haveli of Shree Nathji – Udaipur (Rajasthan)
2. Baithak of Mahaprabhu – Ujjain (M.P.)
3. Temple of Shree Dauji – Kolkkta (W.B.)
4. Haveli of Shree Nathji – Kacha Mandvi (Gujrat)
5. Bhandar of Shree Nathji – Kota (Rajasthan)
6. Baithak of Mahaprabhu – Jagnnathpuri (Orisa)
7. Bhandar of Shree nathji – Jamnagar (Gujarat)
8. Pedi of Shree Nathji - Junagrath (Gujarat)
9. Bhandar of Shree Nathji – Porbandar (Gujarat)
10. Pedi of Shree Nathji - Baroda (Gujrat)
11. Temple of Shree Dauji – Banaras (U.P.)
12. Bhandar of Shree Nathji – Mumbai (Maharastra)
13. Bhandar of Shree Nathji – Mathura (U.P.)
14. Temple of Shree Goverdhan nathji – Lucknow (U.P.)
15. Temple of Shree Goverdhan nathji – Visnagar (U.P.)
16. Baithak of Mahaprabhu – Sidhapur (U.P.)
17. Bhandar of Shree Nathji – Surat (Gujarat)

Eighty four BAITHAKS OF VALLABHACHARYA of Shree Nathji are as under-

1. Gokul (Govindghat)
2. Gokul (In side Temple)
3. Gokul
4. Vrandavan (Near banshivat)
5. Mathura (Vishramghat
6. Madhuvan (Brij)
7. Kumuvan (Brij)
8. Bahulavan (Brij)
9. Shree Radha Kund, Krishan Kund (Brij)
10. Mansi Ganga (Brij)
11. Parsoli (Brij)
12. Anyer (Brij)
13. Govind Kund (Brij)
14. Sundar shila (Near Giriraj, Brij)
15. Giriraj (Brij)
16. Kamvan surabhikund (ShreeKund)
17. Gahvarvan (Barsana)
18. Sanketvan (Brij)
19. Nandgram (Brij)
20. Kokilavan (Brij)
21. Bhandi-van (Brij)
22. Mansarovar (Brij)
23. Sukar Area
24. Chitrakoot-Kamtanath (Kamdegiri)
25. Ayodhaya
26. Nemisharnya
27. Kashi first baithak
28. Kashi second baithak
29. Harihar area (Sonpur)
30. Janakpur
31. Gangasagar sangum
32. Champranya (M.P.)
33. Champranya

34. Jagnnathpuri
35. Pandarpur
36. Nasik
37. Pananrsingh – South
38. Tirupati (Shree Laxmancalaji)
39. Shreerangji
40. Vishnukanchi
41. Setubandh (Rameshvar)
42. Malayachal
43. Lohgragh
44. Tamriparni River
45. Krishna River
46. Pampa sarovar
47. padmanabh
48. Janardan
49. Vidhyanagar (vijainagar)
50. Tilok bhanu
51. Totardi
52. Drbhsharyam
53. Surat
54. Bharuch
55. Morvi
56. Navagagar (Jamnagar)
57. Khambhaliya
58. Pindnarak
59. Mool Gomati
60. Dwaraka
61. Gopi-tailaya (Dwaraka-dham)
62. Shankhodwara
63. Narayan sarovar
64. Junagradh
65. Prabhas
66. Madhavpur
67. Guptaprayag
68. Tagdi
69. Naroda

70. Godhara
71. Kheralu
72. Sidhapur
73. Avantikapuri (Ujjain)
74. Pushakar
75. Kurukshetra
76. Haridwara
77. Badrikasharm
78. Kedarnath
79. Vyavasasharm
80. Himachal Mounthin
81. Vyas ganga
82. Bhardachal
83. Adail
84. Chunar

THE TEMPLE-

Shree Nathji Temple is governed by temple Board act of Rajasthan government. Tilkayat Maharaj is chairman of this board. A senior R.A.S. officer is an executive officer of this board that looks after day-to-day work of the temple.

The Sewa in Shree Nathji temple is of three types

1. Shreeangar 2. Bhog And 3. Rag

In Shreeangar 8 types of cloth and ornaments are dressed on Shree Nath Ji. The names are 1-pag, 2-feta,3-dutmala,4-pga,5-kulhe6-sehra7-tipara8-mukut Apart from these special dresses and ornaments are worn by Shree Nathji

2. Bhog – Every day different times of Bhog are prepared and served to Shree Nathji regularly in all the 8 Darshans

3. Rag – In Shree Nathji temple Kirtan and Bhajans are recited regularly in all the 8 Darshans. Various Ragas are played and Astachap poetry is recited this is known as Haweli Music Dhruvpad is also recited.

Following is a brief layout of the temple.

There are three ways to reach the temple first one is through Chaupati and lal darwaja. From here one can reach to goverdhan chock this opens in Surajpol from Surajpol one can go to Dholipatia from here to Kamal chock and to Doltibari from where one can Darshan Shree Nathji.

The Second route to reach the temple is through Moti Mahal, This rout is near the temple Navneet Priyaji .

The third rout to enter the temple is through Preetampole, This rout is near Rasoi ghar through this one can reach to Dholipatia for Darshan.

There is no Shikhar in the temple , the whole temple is Pakka constricted but the place where Shree Nathji Swaroop is placed is made up of Khaprel(Kacha)

Sudrashan Chakra Raj is flying with 7 coloured Dhawaja. The sudrashan Chakra is daily scented and every pilgrim worships the chakra.

The temple has following sections 1. Kharch Bhandar 2. Shree Krishn Bhandar 3. Dholi Patia 4. Library 5. Kamal Chock 6. Ratan Chowk 7. Doll –tibari 8. Anarwala Chowk 9. Khasa Bhandar 10. Prasadi- Bhandar 11. Sudarshan- chakra 12. Shakaghar 13. Panghar 14. Phoolghar 15. doodhghar 16. Mishreeghar 17. Padaghar 18. Patalghar 19. Mani-Kotha 20. Rasoighar 21. Lalaji Ka Mandir 22. Navnit Priyaji Ka Bagicha

Other Pusti Margi temples in Shree Nathdwara
1. Temple of Shree Navnitpriyaji
2. Temple of Shree Vitthalnathji
3. Temple of Shree Vanmalilalji

4. Temple of Shree Kalayanraiji
5. Baithak of Shree Gokulnathji
6. Temple of Shree Madanmohanlalji
7. Temple of Shree Yamunanikunj

NAMES OF UTSAVS IN SHREENATHJI TEMPLE

1. Manorath-Fullday
2. Manorath of Mangla
3. Manorath of Rajbhog – This can be done in half and quarter amount also
4. Manorath of Shayanbhog

Image-Cow playing game on Deepawali

Apart from above mentioned Manorath the following Manorath can also be performad.
      i. navotsava
     ii. Golden Hindola
    iii. 56 Bhog
    iv. Attarbhog
     v. Samagri
    vi. Chandanl Bangla
   vii. Hantdi of Silver
  viii. Kali shreengar
    ix. Janmastmi
     x. Nandmahostva
    xi. Dipawali
   xii. Annakuta
  xiii. Flowermandli

The rates of these above mentioned manoraths can be obtained from the temple office. The Prasad (food) of Shreenathji is of two types
1. The sakari prasad
2. The unsakari prasad

The sakari prasad includes rice, roti, bati, zeera puri, pakori, thapadi, khir, khichadi, shreekhand, dahi, mango juice, rabadi, meva bhat, dahi bhat, seera, churma, rayata, achar, murabba, curi and various green vegetables.

The unsakari prasad includes milk, makkhan, badam ka seera, shak ghar ki barfi, dudh ghar burfi, dudh puri, magah sattu and churama ladooh, thore mathadi, rajbhog ki puri, tava puri, ghevar, julabi, mohan thal, mesu pak, badam pak, rabadi malai, dahi. These bhog prasad are distributed to various employs of shreenathji.

The prasad of sheenath ji can be obtained from the temple office after depositing the required amount. Recently the prasasd is also sent by currier and by speed post. The pilgrims can also purchased the prasad from shopkeepers. The temple board has its own shops. The best prasad of shreenath ji is known as sobhagya soth. The cost of burfi is very high. Similarly in nav utsav 1.25 lakhs mangoes are used as prasad. Pan is also an important item for shreenath ji. Katha, chuna and supari is also very special. The pan is known as beera. Costly item like kesar, kasturi, amber, baras are regularly used in prasad and for grinding golden and silver hand-mills are used. Peda of pili mitti with Yamuna river water is also distributed regularly. The prasad of shreenath ji goes not only to all part of the country but also to various foreign countries.

The Darshan timing are as follows

1. Mangala	5.30 am
2. Shreengar	7 to 7.15 am
3. Gwal	8.45 to 9.00am
4. Rajbhogh	10.45 to 11.30am
5. Uthapan	3.30 to 3.45pm
6. Bhog	4.15 to 4.30pm
7. Arti	5.15 to 5.30pm
8. Shayan	6.30 to 7.00pm

The timings are approximate and variable. Any person can go to darshan of Shreenathji ,all vaishanvas wear a tulsi mala in neck.

sewa of Shree Nathji is of two types – Name -sewa and Sawroop sewa, The Swaroop sewa is of three types – Tanuja, (physical) Vitja, (financial) and Mansi (mental). All these sewas are included in Pustimarg . Lord Shree Nathji is in nitya lila in the temple.

The budget of the temple is governed by the temple board, large number of gifts in cash and kind are received every day in the temple .Sender Shree Nathji, receiver Shree Nathji is a common proverb here.

Main Tourist spots in Shree Nathdwara are:

1. Moti Mahal
2. Dhruve Window
3. Standing Ganeshji

4. Bada–Mangra- represents the Goverdhan of Brij
5. Lal bagh and Palaces
6. Vrindavan Bagh
7. Banas river- This represents the Holly Yamunaji
8. Palaces of Gangore Ghat on Banas
9. Ganesh Tekri
10. Kachvai Garden
11. Goshala at Nathuvas
12. Sahitya Mandal
13. Vidya Vibhag

In Shree Nathdwara following are old water–bodies
1. Banas river
2. Sunder vilas
3. Krishana-Kund
4. Nathuvas lake
5. Girdhar Sagar
6. Siyad lake
7. Ahilya Kund
8. Vyas Kund
9. Govind Sarover

In Shree Nathdwara there are wrestling places for the development of youth viz. Mobe-Gargh, Ambavada, Gondavada, Naya Akhada etc.

Tourist Spots around Shree Nathdwara

- Kankroli- 16 Kilometer from Shree Nathdwara is situated Dwarka Nathji temple. Rajsamand lake and Nine Chowkis are spots of importance.

- Ek Lingji Mahadev – On Udaipur route is Situated Ek ling Mahadevji Temple of Mewar Maharana. There is a lake and Sash-Bahu Temple.

Udaipur – 50 K.M. from Shree Nathdwara is famous Udaipur the capital of Mewar State. There are several spots like Moti Dungri, Sahaliyon ki Bari, City palace, Pichola and Fateh Sagar Lake. One can boat also.

- Haldi Ghati – 20 K.M. from Shree Nathdwara is Haldi Ghati the famous Battle-Place where King Akabar and Maharana Pratap fought the battle. Chetak Samadhi is also a good Historical spot.

- Ghassyar – This is near Shree Nathdwara and there is a small Temple of Shree Nathji.

- Shree Char Bhujaji – 65 K.M. from Shree Nathdwara is

Shree Char Bhujaji where lord Vishnu is in his four arms Swaroop.

- Kumbhal Gargh – 90 K.M. from Shree Nathdwara is famous Kumhal Garh forth Constructed by Maharana Kumbha.

rajsamand lake

- Chittore – Chittore is famous capital of Mewar state. The town has various spots. Sanwaraji Temple is also very famous place. Avarimata Temple should also be visited. Bhadesar is also a good spot.

- Mount abu – Is famous hill station of Rajasthan and has so many spots.

- Jain Temples of Ranakpur

- 11 Molela-a small village near shree Nathdwara is famous for terracotta art work. The terracotta artists of Molela prepare various statues of Gods by hand and they are sold to Gujarat, Madhaya - Pradesh and foreign countries. A70 m long terracotta has been exhibited in jaipur. Molela is 11 Km from Shree Nathdwara.

- Marble Industry-In recent years mining of marbles, cutting and trading has become a good business in Shree Nathdwara and surrounding areas. A development plan of Shree Nathdwara town is in process and temple board is managing it.

Market, colonies –The main markets of Shree Nathdwara are as under

1- Mandir market
2-Naya bazar
3-Chaupati
4-Delhi bazar
5-Gandhi road
6- Sabji bazar
7-nai sadak
8-lal bazar
9-bora bazar
10-telipura
11-bus stand
12-lal bagh

There are many colonies in Shree Nathdwara-they are
1-gurjarpura,2-lodha ghati3- parikrama4-imli ka chowk5-bichu magari 6-tailion katalab7-mohan garh8-setho ka mohalla9-mochiwada10-brijpura 11-fauj mohalla12- siyad 13-lal bagh 14-nathuvas15- sukhadia nagar16- sidhi colony 17-kumhar pada18-nai haweli19-shriji colony20-yadav mohalla21-vallabh pura22-jarana colony23-ram pura24-tahsil road 25-bus stand colony.

The day to day manage ment of town is managed by nagar palika.

There are many temples of lord shiva, Ganeshji, Hanumanji, mataji, bheruji, ramji; krishnaji at various places for vershiping.masjid is also there.

The town has very rich cultural heritage. All types of festivals are celebrated by the citizens.Hindi,mevadi,brij,langvages are spoken.Music,art and culture, are loved by all.katha –vachan of sri madbhgvat ,ramayan .geeta is a regular feature in the holly town here.

All festivals of all castes are celebrated by all citizens. There are a large number of educational institutes for the benefit of new generation.

Brahmans,jains,bhils,,rajputs,muslims, other backward classes,yadavs etc. live in the town with a communal harmony. Dipawali ,holi, ed,Krishna janmastmi,nand – utsav,dashara,annakutotsva,sharadotsava,chhapan bhog utsav ,maker sankranti, are commonly celebrated.

PLACES TO STAY IN SHREE NATHDWARA
1. Dheeraj Dham:
2. New cottage
3. Vallbha cottage
1. Dak Bungalow
2. Kothari Dharmshala
6. Utsav Hotel
7. Vandana hotel
8. Chanda Bhai ki dharmshala
9. Delhi wali dharmshala
10. Asu Bhai ki dharmshala
11. Choti dharmshala
12. Delwara wali dharmshala
13. Bambai wali (Badi) dharmshala
14. Mani Bahi ki dharmshala
15. Basanji Lalji ki dharmshala
16. Nai sethani ki dharmshala
17. Sindhi wali dharmshala
18. Keshav Bhawan
19. Daya Bhawan
20. Telipura wali dharmshala
21. Gopallal ki dharmshala
22. Badi sethani ki dharmshala
23. Madan MohanLal ki dharmshala
24. Laxmi niwas dharmshala
25. Vanma li lalji ki dharmshala
26. Vitthalnathji ki dharmshala

Stay facilities are also available at Kankroli ,Udaipur and chittore. Resorts are also available on National highway.

Politicians, journalists, writers ,musicians of Shree Nathdwara

Politicians of Shree Nathdwara – Mohan lal Sukhadia, Master Kishan lal, Ganesh lal Sanchihar, Narender pal singh chaudhari, Navneet Paliwal, Manohar Kothari, Fateh lal Bapu, Dr. Girja vyas, Dr. C.P. Joshi, kalyan singh,Shivdan singh chauhan are main politicians of Shree Nathdwara and have served the country for a long time. A Large No. of freedom fighters has been residing in Shree Nathdwara .

DR.C.P.JOSHI   DR.GIRIJA VYAS

Mohan lal sukhadia served as a chief minister of Rajasthan for sixteen years. At present dr.-prof. C.P.JOSHI is central cabinet minister for rural development and panchayati raj.Dr.girija vyas is chair person of national women commission.

Regarding journalism,babu Bhartendu Harish chander lived here for some time and worked.Bal krishan Sharma navin also lived here.Bhagwati Prasad devpura,Manohar kothari,Navneet paliwal,B.L.Joshi, Prabhu das vairagi, Ragunath, yashwant kothari are few writers known out side. .Brij bhasha,rajasthani is also spoken and poets are writing in these languages also.

A large number of budding writers and journalists are coming up.

A large number of musicians had lived in the town .The list includes Harnathji,Purushottamji,Ramdasji, Mannalalji,shyam lalji,Amritlalji , Pannalalji,prakash kumavat . These persons played haveli music in temple, they also recite on radio and TV.

The town has many famous educationists also. Anadilalji shastri,yasvant lal nagar,girdharji,Shivsagari, Gorisanker shukla tilkeshji ,Bhagwati Prasad devpura and many others have shaped the future of new generation.

The town has many astrologers .Onkarlalji, sukdevji, jamnalalji , bal devji are a few to name.

References

1. Wall Paintings –Meera Seth – Publications Division, ministry of information and broad casting, government of India-New Delhi.
2. Rajasthani Rag-mala chitra parampara- SuMahendra- Publications scheme, Jaipur.
3. India in colours- Mulk Raj Anand- Tarapore Wala and sons- Mumbai.
4. Artists of Nathdwara- Trynelyones
5. Paintings of Nathdwara- SPAN, July 1970, USIS New Delhi.
6. Sri Nathdwara Ka Sanskritic Itihas- Prabhu Das Vairagi- Bharat Prakashan Mandir, Aligargh (U.P.)
7. Heerak Jayanti Granth- Sahitya Mandal- Nathdwara (Rajasthan)
8. Heerak Jayanti Supplementary granth Sahitya Mandal, Nathdwara (Rajasthan).
9. Nathdwara-Darshan-Bhagwati Prasad Devpura-Satyesh Pustak Bhandar, Nathdwara (Rajasthan).
10. Rajasthan Ki Sanskritic Parampra-Jai Singh Neeraj et al-Rajasthan Hindi Granth Academy, Jaipur.
11. Rajasthan Ka Sanskritic Itihas-Dr. Gopi Nath Sharma-Rajasthan Hindi Granth Academy, Jaipur.
12. Rajasthan Vaibhav-T.N. Chaturvedi et al-Bhartiya Sanskriti Sanrakshan Avam Samvardhan Parishad, New Delhi.
13. Bhartiya Swantrya Andolan Ka Itihas- Government of Rajasthan Publication.
14. Srimad Vallabhacharya Charit- Krishna Chand Shastri.
15. Chaurasi Vaishnavon Ki Varta.
16. Mahaprabhu Sri Vallabha Charya-Seth Govind Das.

17. Rajputana-Ka Itihas-Gori Shanker-Heerachand Ojha.
18. History of Rajasthan-Colonel James Todd.
19. SriNathdwara Ka Itihas-Krishnachand Shastri.
20. Harish Chandra Mohan Chandrika-Bhartendu Babu Harish Chandra Sundarshan Yantralaya, Nathdwara.
21. Bhartendu-Samagra-Hemant Sharma-Hindi Pracharak Sans than Varanasi(U.P.)
22. Later Mewar-Ram Vallabh Somani.
23. Kala-Bhumi-Rajasthan-Yashwant Kothari-Rastradoot 3-4-1988,Jaipur.
24. Krishna-Upasana-Yashwant Kothari Rastriya-Sahara-Delhi.
25. Rajasthan Ki Lagu Chitra Shailiya-Rajasthan Lalit Kala Academy Jaipur.
26. Murti Kala-Rai Krishan Das
27. Pichvai Kala Of Nathdwara-Yashwant Kothari-Rastradoot-3-4-1988
28 Brija SANKRITI KA ITIHAS --VANKTESHWARA Press MUMBAI
29SHREE VALLABHA PUSTI Prakash Mumbai
30Brija ka itihas Part 1-2 K.D. Vajpai
31 Brija Ke Dharma asampradaya ka itihas -PRAbhu D AYAL
32sriDwarka NATH KA PRAKTYA –Vidya vibhag Kankroli
33shreeNATHJI KI PRAKTYA VARTA vidya vibhag Nathdwara

34ASTA Chapaa Samrti Granth –Sahitya MANDAL Nathdwara

35 Shree Nathji ank- Sahitya Mandal Nathdwara
36 Hamere Pujya Tirth- Pustak Mahal ,Dehli

37 Rajasthani Temple Hanging of the Krishana Cult- Calico Mill Publication

38 Shree Krishana & Shree Nath Ji- Amit Amba lal, Ahemdabad

39 On Visiting Nathdwara-Nilima Shankh

oooooooooooooooooooooooo

Made in the USA
Columbia, SC
16 April 2021